W9-BZG-188

GROUSE

Tim Harris

Grolier
an imprint of

www.scholastic.com/librarypublishing

Published 2008 by Grolier
An imprint of Scholastic Library Publishing
Old Sherman Turnpike, Danbury,
Connecticut 06816

For The Brown Reference Group plc
Project Editor: Jolyon Goddard
Copy-editors: Lesley Ellis, Lisa Hughes,
    Wendy Horobin
Picture Researcher: Clare Newman
Designers: Jeni Child, Lynne Ross,
    Sarah Williams
Managing Editor: Bridget Giles

Volume ISBN-13: 978-0-7172-6236-6
Volume ISBN-10: 0-7172-6236-7

**Library of Congress
Cataloging-in-Publication Data**

Nature's children. Set 1.
    p. cm.
Includes index.
ISBN-13: 978-0-7172-8080-3
ISBN-10: 0-7172-8080-2
1. Animals--Encyclopedias, Juvenile.
QL49.N38 2007
590--dc22

                2007018359

Printed and bound in China

PICTURE CREDITS

Front Cover: Nature PL: Markus Varesvuo.

Back Cover: Nature PL: Yuri Shibnev, Igor
Shpilenok, David Tipling, Markus Varesvuo.

Alamy: Andy Thompson 45; **Ardea**: Tom
& Pat Leeson 33; **Corbis**: W. Perry Conway
1, 46, Darrell Gulin 26/27, D. Robert &
Lorri Franz 4, 21; **FLPA**: David Hosking 18,
Mark Newman 17, Konrad Wothe / Minden
Pictures 34; **Nature PL**: Shattil & Rozinski
5, Steve Knell 37, Artur Tabot 42; **NHPA**:
Jari Peltomaki 10, Andy Rouse 3, 14;
Photolibrary.com: C. C. Lockwood 22;
Photos.com: 13; **Shutterstock**: Muriel
Lasure 29, Janis Strausmanis 6; **Still
Pictures**: C. Allen Morgan 30;
Superstock: 41, Tom Brakefield 9, 38.

Contents

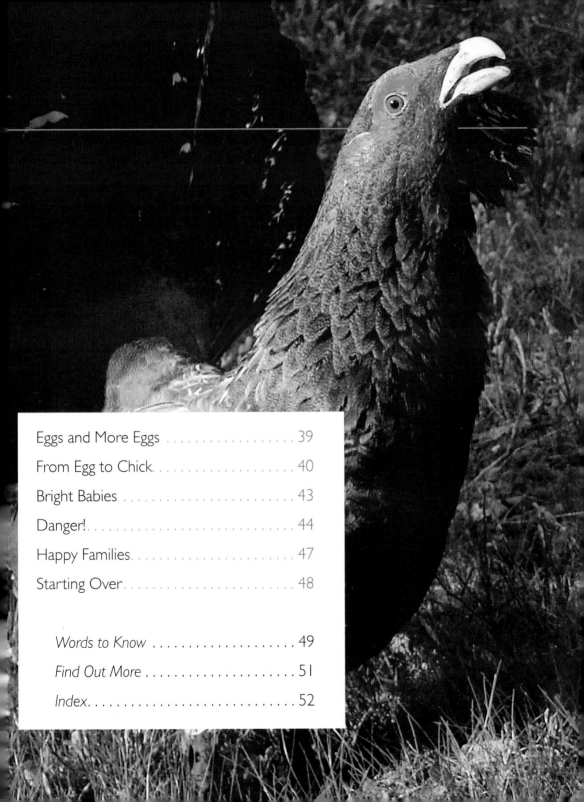

FACT FILE: Grouse

Class	Birds (Aves)
Order	Chickenlike birds (Galliformes)
Family	Grouse family (Phasianidae)
Genera	Worldwide many; seven in North America
Species	There are 11 species of North American grouse (about 130 subspecies worldwide)
World distribution	On every continent, apart from Antarctica
Habitat	Forest, tundra, and grassland
Distinctive physical characteristics	Grouse differ from the other chickenlike birds by having feathers that partly or completely cover their legs
Habits	Grouse spend most of their time on the ground; they often stand completely still if a predator is detected; female birds (hens) try to lead predators away from their chicks
Diet	Shoots, buds, berries; varies with species

Introduction

Where do grouse live? Not in trees, like many other birds. Grouse live on the ground. That is where they find most of their food, and that is where they build their nests and raise their young. Grouse have a short beak, short legs, and a head that is small compared to the size of its body. Their tail has a rounded shape when it is spread. All grouse can fly, but they are not strong fliers.

Most grouse have lots of brown and gray feathers. Some grouse change their color dramatically in fall. Sometimes the males, or **cocks**, are brighter than the females, or **hens**.

During the breeding season, a male prairie chicken (right) has noticeable yellow patches on his head.

The capercaillie is the largest member of the grouse family.

All Sizes Available

Grouse come in many sizes. Some grouse are small and others are large. The white-tailed ptarmigan (TAR-MI-GUN) is North America's smallest grouse. It is only 12 inches (30 cm) long and weighs just 13 ounces (360 g). That's about the same weight as a large baking potato.

The biggest grouse of all is the capercaillie (KA-PUR-KAY-LEE), which lives in the pine forests of northern Europe and Asia. A capercaillie looks a little like a wild turkey and is almost as heavy. If you put a male capercaillie on one end of a see-saw, you would need about 12 ptarmigans to balance it!

Male grouse are often heavier than the females. Male sage-grouse are twice as heavy as their mates. A male capercaillie is about three times heavier than a female capercaillie.

Grouse Habitats

Grouse live in most parts of North America and many other regions of the world. The type of place where a grouse lives is called its **habitat**. Spruce grouse, ruffed grouse, and blue grouse live in forests. Willow ptarmigan and rock ptarmigan prefer to live in the treeless arctic **tundra**. The two types of sage-grouse live only on dry sagebrush plains. Sharp-tailed grouse and—as their name suggests—prairie-chickens live on **prairies**. Prairies are large grasslands.

In fact, there aren't many areas of North America where grouse do not live. The ruffed grouse is the most common grouse. It even lives in small woodlands and ravines near some big cities. A word of warning: if you go out looking for grouse, be patient because they are often hard to see.

A ruffed grouse looks for food in a conifer tree.

9

In winter you may have to look hard to spot a hazel grouse in a tree.

Camouflage Colors

Grouse have plenty of enemies, or **predators**, that would love to catch them and eat them for dinner. So it is for a good reason that grouse have protective coloring that helps them blend in with their surroundings. This ability to merge with their background is called **camouflage**.

The color of a grouse's feathers depends on where the bird lives. The feathers may be dark brown, gray, red, or a mixture of these colors. Often, each dark feather has a paler edge, making it look like a leaf or pebble. The blue grouse has dusky bluish gray feathers. This color blends well with the bird's mountain home.

Show-off Colors

Grouse don't want to be seen most of the time. At the start of the **breeding season**, however, male grouse show off bright feathers that are hidden at other times of the year. They show off to attract the attention of the female grouse.

Some males have bright red markings over each eye. On blue grouse, these marks are yellow. Male sage-grouse have long feathers, called **filoplumes** (FEE-LOH-PLOOMS), growing from the back of their head.

When male spruce grouse spread their tail feathers, they reveal either a bold yellow band or bright white spots. Male prairie-chickens have bright reddish or yellow-orange feathers on the sides of their neck. These feathers are displayed only when the birds are showing off to females.

A male sage-grouse with spiky tail feathers struts to impress the hens.

13

An alarmed red
grouse takes off.

Flying Grouse

Grouse can fly, but they are awkward at taking off. They are more likely to make their escape from predators on foot rather than by flying away. People sometimes see a grouse only for it to "disappear," never to be seen again. On the open tundra, rock ptarmigan slip silently behind rocks to hide. In forests, ruffed grouse walk quietly into thick cover to make their escape. Ruffed grouse are also good climbers. They can climb up the thin, flexible stems of bushes.

Willow ptarmigan often fly when danger approaches. But because their wings are not very large, and they are heavy birds, they cannot fly high, nor very far. Their wings beat so fast that they look like a blur.

Buds and Bugs

You wouldn't find it much fun if you had to eat a grouse's diet. They feed on young grass shoots, other leaves, the buds of shrubs, seeds, berries, and a few twigs. Grouse **chicks** have a bit more variety in what they eat. They swallow flies, beetles, ants, and spiders, as well as plant material. However, as they get older they eat fewer and fewer bugs.

Some grouse eat almost the same thing all the time. The capercaillie, a large grouse that lives in Europe and Asia, eats the needles of pine and other conifer trees and—if they are available—berries. Although that may seem like a very boring diet, capercaillies get more energy from each beakful of pine needles than they could from anything else they might eat.

A spruce grouse chomps on a tasty plant shoot.

A blue grouse hen swallows small stones that she finds on a road.

Stony Stomachs

Before grouse can get all the goodness out of their food, it has to be broken into small pieces. But how do grouse mash up their food? After all, they eat sharp pine needles, really tough leaves, and hard twigs—and they don't have teeth! Grouse and other birds "chew" their food in a special stomach called the **gizzard**. The gizzard has a tough inner lining, which grinds up the bird's food.

Sometimes, early in the morning, grouse can be seen at the side of the road, picking up and swallowing small stones. These stones collect in the gizzard, where they help mash up pine needles and other tough plant food.

Grouse Snowshoes

Have you ever tried walking through snow wearing ordinary shoes? It's slow progress, isn't it? But with snowshoes, which spread out your weight and keep you from sinking into the snow, it is much easier. Grouse spend most of their time on the ground, and many of them live in places where the snow piles high in winter. But that is not a problem for them.

In winter, most grouse grow a fringe of scales along each toe. These scales increase the area of each foot, so the bird's weight is spread out more evenly. That keeps the grouse from sinking into the snow.

Some ptarmigans, such as the willow ptarmigan, white-tailed ptarmigan, and rock ptarmigan, have an even better way of getting around in the snow—and keeping their feet warm at the same time. They make their feet bigger by growing warm feathers on them. The feathers stop the bird from sinking far into the snow.

The feathery feet
of the white-tailed
ptarmigan stop
the bird from
sinking too far
into snow.

A ruffed grouse's head peeps out from its snowy hideaway.

Snow Beds

Grouse do not fly south in fall as many other birds do. They do not curl up and go to sleep for winter as bears and squirrels do. These birds live outside all through winter and have to put up with freezing weather. Of course, grouse have nice warm feathers that keep them from getting too cold most of the time. But even feathers can't keep them warm on the coldest nights.

Grouse have an amazing solution: they sleep in holes in the snow! Although a snow bed would be too cold for us, it can be warmer than the outside air. So on a winter evening, ruffed grouse fly down from where they have been feeding in the trees. Then, they burrow head first into a nearby snowbank. The ruffed grouse stay there until the following morning.

Changing Color

Ptarmigans live in an open habitat called tundra. The tundra landscape is a mixture of browns, greens, and grays—the colors of the grasses and rocks. In spring and fall the grasses and rocks are partly covered by snow. During winter snow blankets the whole ground. So how do ptarmigans remain camouflaged when the color of the landscape changes with the seasons? The birds change, or **molt**, their feathers in spring and fall to match their surroundings!

In spring, they grow patterned brown, gray, and white feathers that match the colors of the tundra perfectly. In fall, these feathers are replaced by an almost all-white coat, which blends in with the snow. In spring and fall, while the new feathers are gradually replacing the old ones, the birds are a mix of white and gray-brown. These colors match the pattern of patchy snow in spring and fall.

24

Fly or Freeze?

Grouse do not have hooked beaks or sharp claws to fight off predators. They try to avoid fights with their enemies. There are two things grouse can do if an enemy approaches. They can stay dead-still and pretend they are not there, relying on their camouflage to keep them hidden. Or they can fly away.

First, grouse must be aware that a predator—a fox or a hawk—is in the area. Grouse do not have a good sense of smell. They use their eyes and ears to detect enemies. Even the slightest noise will alert them to danger. Their eyes can see even tiny, distant movements. Once they have seen or heard something suspicious, the grouse have to decide whether to fly or freeze.

The willow ptarmigan's colors keep it hidden and safe from hungry predators.

Noisy Show-offs

Every year during the breeding season, grouse mate and raise families. Before they can mate, male and female grouse have to pair up. In spring, each male claims an area of land as his own. This area is called his territory. The male then puts on a show to attract females.

These shows, or **courtship displays**, begin early in the spring, sometimes when there is still snow on the ground. They last for several weeks. Often they end when the male has attracted a female. But a male doesn't always succeed in convincing a hen to be his partner, and he might give up.

Each kind of grouse has its own courtship display. Some are amazing to watch. Others are very hard for people to see because the birds are hidden in the forest. But whatever the display, courting males are usually very noisy!

A male blue grouse inflates the red sacks on his neck to impress hens.

A male greater prairie-chicken booms during courtship displays.

Prairie Boomers

Have you ever blown over the top of an empty bottle? The resulting noise sounds like a low, hooting moan. That is just like the noise male greater prairie-chickens make when they are performing their **booming** display. Their booms carry far across the open grasslands where they live.

Male prairie-chickens strut backward and forward in front of each other. They raise their neck feathers around two orange pouches on their breast. The birds suck air into these pouches, then send it rushing out in a series of loud booms.

In spring, up to 20 male prairie-chickens display at the same place. Each cock, or male, tries to impress the females. Every so often the males push and shove at each other, trying to get to the middle of the group. There, they can show off best.

Is it a Motorcycle?

If you go for a springtime walk in some parts of North America, you might hear something very strange. Even though you are a long way from a road, it sounds just like a powerful motorcycle engine starting up: "Dud... dud... dud... dud... du-du-du-du-du-du." Confused? It might be the sound of a male ruffed grouse displaying to attract a female.

To make this noise, the male stands on top of a favorite log and beats the air with his wings. At the end of a series of "drums," his wings are pumping so fast they are just a blur. When he stops, he fans his tail, raises his dark neck feathers and stands quietly for a few minutes. Then he performs the show all over again. In the middle of the day male ruffed grouse feed. They display again in the evening.

A male ruffed grouse displays by "drumming" his wings.

Who will be top
in the pecking
order? Male black
grouse fight it out.

Fighting Grouse

Black grouse are the real show-offs. They put
on one of the most amazing displays of all birds.
Every spring up to 200 male birds gather in one
place to attract females. This gathering is called
a **lek**. Some leks have happened at the same
place for more than 50 years.

Each male fans out his tail so it forms a bright
white semicircle. The male defends his place
in the lek, hissing and making other noises.
Rival males approach each other, jump off
the ground, and peck each other. While that
is happening, the female grouse walk past,
checking out each male in turn. Those males
that are near the center of the lek have the most
success attracting the females. Why that is, no
one knows for sure.

A Nest for the Eggs

After they have mated, most female grouse build a nest in a hollow on the ground. That is where she will lay her eggs. The position of the nest is very important. If the eggs are discovered by a hungry animal, they will be eaten. If the eggs get too cold, the growing chicks inside will die.

The grouse hen chooses a place that is hidden from view, protected from cold winds, and not likely to flood if it rains. Popular places are at the base of a tree or large rock or by a log or brush pile. The most simple grouse nests are just bits of earth and stones scraped into a rough circle. Others are built of leaves, sticks, pine needles, and feathers.

A rock ptarmigan hen makes a nest on the ground.

A ruffed grouse hen keeps a watchful eye on her chicks and eggs.

Eggs and More Eggs

The total number of eggs a mother grouse lays is called a **clutch**. She lays one egg a day. The clutch may have as few as 5 eggs, as many as 17, or any number in between. The eggs are usually cream colored or yellow with brown or reddish streaks or blotches. The rock ptarmigan lays red eggs, but they fade to yellow-brown after a few days. These colors help the eggs blend in with the surroundings so they cannot be seen.

If she ate well during the late winter, the mother grouse is more likely to lay more eggs. Sometimes black grouse nests contain even more eggs. That is probably because two females have laid eggs in the same place. If a predator takes a whole clutch of eggs, the mother sometimes lays another clutch.

From Egg to Chick

A mother grouse sits on her eggs to keep them warm. That is called **incubation** and it is very important: if an egg gets cold, the growing chick within dies. Every day, the hen turns the eggs with her beak so that they remain warm on all sides. It doesn't harm the eggs if she leaves them for a short while, but she must not desert them for a long period. Unlike many birds, the father grouse does not help the mother incubate the eggs.

The eggs incubate for about three weeks. Then, the chicks inside peck a ring of holes around the large end of their egg. The chicks use a bump on their tiny beak called an **egg tooth** to force their way out. They begin to call their mother even before they have broken out of the egg. Then they force their way out into the world.

A ptarmigan chick begins to break out of its egg.

A capercaillie chick
waits for its mother.

Bright Babies

Apart from being tiny, newborn grouse are nothing like other baby birds. They are neither blind nor helpless. They are covered with soft, downy feathers and leave the nest within an hour of hatching. A very short time later they can run almost as fast as their parents.

Although grouse chicks are smart baby birds, they still need help from their mother. They follow their mother, who shows them what they should be eating. Grouse chicks eat insects as well as buds, leaves, and berries.

Danger!

Life can be dangerous for grouse chicks when they are very small. If the chicks follow their mother's example, they have a much better chance of survival.

The mother lets her babies know where she is all the time by quietly calling to them. Predators are a constant danger. Birds of prey such as hawks and small mammals such as weasels will grab and kill a grouse chick given half a chance. If the mother makes a high-pitched call, the chicks know that there is danger nearby. The chicks "freeze" like statues until the threat has passed.

Another danger is not so obvious. Grouse chicks may die if they become too cold. So sometimes they huddle close to their mother to take advantage of her warmth. Once warmed, they're off in search of food again.

A red grouse
mother is always
on the lookout
for danger.

45

White-tailed ptarmigans team up in winter to find food.

Happy Families

Chicks must eat throughout the day. And all this eating pays off: chicks double in weight in the week after they hatch. Grouse families feed mostly in the mornings and evenings. They may rest in a safe place in the afternoon. Usually, the father lives alone and does not stay with his **brood**, or offspring. However, male willow ptarmigans do stay with their family and help protect the chicks by attacking any enemy.

Some grouse chicks can fly when they are as young as 10 days. Others are three or four weeks old before they can get airborne. But they remain with their mother until the fall. By then they are able to look after themselves. They have warm feathers and know where to find food. That is the time when most grouse families break up.

Young grouse may team up with other grouse during winter. Or they may spend winter alone. This is a difficult time of year because food is often harder to find than in summer and fall.

Starting Over

When the weather begins to get warmer, the snow melts on the tundra, new buds grow in the forest, and new grass grows on the prairie. Food is much easier to find. The grouse that have survived the winter can now eat and put on weight. Even though they are less than a year old, some of the previous year's young males will set up a territory and start displaying to attract a mate. Other grouse will wait until the following year before they pair up.

Soon the sound of displaying grouse will be replaced by silence as the hens lay eggs and the chicks begin to hatch.

Words to Know

Booming Low, hooting moans made by male greater prairie-chickens.

Breeding season The time of the year animals come together to have young.

Brood Young birds that grow up together.

Camouflage Coloring or markings that help an animal blend in with its surroundings.

Chick Young grouse.

Clutch A group of eggs.

Cock Male grouse.

Courtship display Behavior used to attract a mate or claim a territory.

Egg tooth Toothlike point on the end of a chick's beak used to break out of the egg.

Filoplume	Long feather growing from the back of a cock's head.
Gizzard	A stomach with a tough inner lining that grinds food.
Habitat	A place where an animal or plant lives, such as a grassland or a forest.
Hen	Female grouse.
Incubation	Sitting on eggs and keeping them warm so the chicks inside can grow.
Lek	A gathering of male birds.
Molt	To shed feathers and grow new ones.
Prairies	Large grasslands with few trees.
Predators	Animals that hunt other animals.
Tundra	Icy and treeless land in the far north.

Find Out More

Books

Furtman, M. *Ruffed Grouse: Woodland Drummer.*
Harrisburg, Pennsylvania: Stackpole Books, 2004.

London, J. *Gone Again Ptarmigan.* Washington, DC:
National Geographic Children's Books, 2001.

Web sites

Alaska Department of Fish and Game: Grouse
www.adfg.state.ak.us/pubs/notebook/bird/grouse.php
Facts about Alaska's blue grouse, spruce grouse, ruffed
grouse, and sharp-tailed grouse.

All About Birds
www.birds.cornell.edu/AllAboutBirds/BirdGuide/
Information about all the species of grouse and
ptarmigans found in North America.

Index